CANOEING

BY SARA GREEN

BELLWETHER MEDIA • MINNEAPOLIS, MN

Jump into the cockpit and take flight with Pilot books. Your journey will take you on high-energy adventures as you learn about all that is wild, weird, fascinating, and fun!

This edition first published in 2013 by Bellwether Media, Inc.

No part of this publication may be reproduced in whole or in part without written permission of the publisher. For information regarding permission, write to Bellwether Media, Inc., Attention: Permissions Department, 5357 Penn Avenue South, Minneapolis, MN 55419.

Library of Congress Cataloging-in-Publication Data

Green, Sara, 1964-
Canoeing / by Sara Green.
    p. cm. – (Pilot books: outdoor adventures)
Includes bibliographical references and index.
Summary: "Engaging images accompany information about canoeing. The combination of high-interest subject matter and narrative text is intended for students in grades 3 through 7"–Provided by publisher.
ISBN 978-1-60014-795-1 (hardcover : alk. paper)
 1. Canoes and canoeing–Juvenile literature. I. Title.
GV784.3.G74 2012
797.122–dc23   2012015006

Printed in the United States of America, North Mankato, MN.

TABLE OF CONTENTS

AN EVENING PADDLE

A calm, glassy lake reflects the trees that line the shore. Two people push a canoe into the water and climb in. One sits in the stern, ready to steer. The other sits in the bow. The canoe glides along the edge of the lake as they dip their paddles into the water.

The canoeists look around for wildlife. A fish jumps out of the water in front of them. A turtle basking on a log plops into the water when the canoe gets too close. Overhead, a bald eagle soars in the sky. Later, as the sun begins to set, the canoeists paddle back to shore.

Canoeing is a popular outdoor recreational activity. Many canoeists enjoy spending a few hours on a quiet lake. Others prefer to go on canoeing adventures that last several days. Either way, canoeing offers people the chance to relax on the water and experience the outdoors.

Canoes are narrow boats with pointed ends. The body of a canoe is called the hull. The top edge is called the gunwale. The thwarts are supports that extend from one side of the canoe to the other. One or two people use paddles to move a canoe through the water.

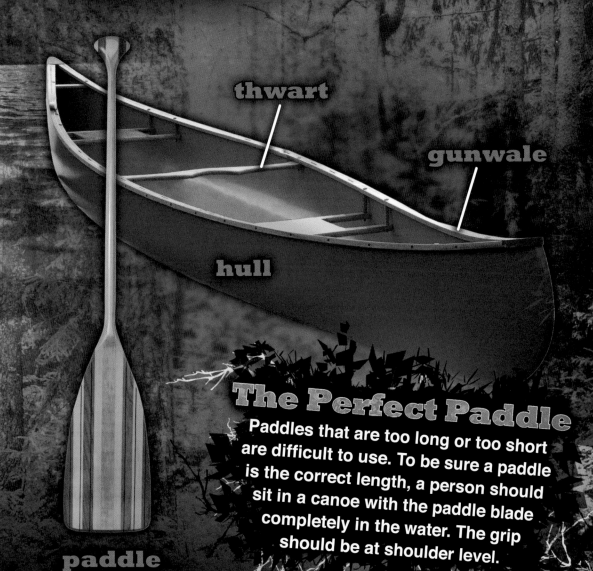

thwart

gunwale

hull

paddle

The Perfect Paddle

Paddles that are too long or too short are difficult to use. To be sure a paddle is the correct length, a person should sit in a canoe with the paddle blade completely in the water. The grip should be at shoulder level.

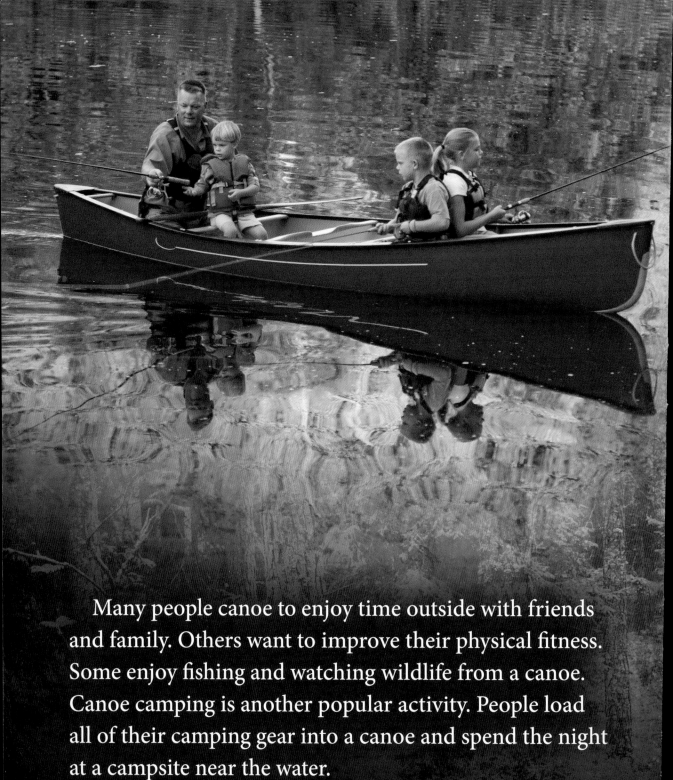

Many people canoe to enjoy time outside with friends and family. Others want to improve their physical fitness. Some enjoy fishing and watching wildlife from a canoe. Canoe camping is another popular activity. People load all of their camping gear into a canoe and spend the night at a campsite near the water.

Canoes can also be used in races and on rushing rivers. Races feature teams of one or two canoeists. They take place on lakes, rivers, and even oceans. Some races are over 100 miles (160 kilometers) long! Whitewater canoeists paddle short canoes in fast-moving water. These canoes are easier to steer and can make quick, tight turns. Some brave whitewater canoeists take their canoes down small waterfalls!

CANOES AND EQUIPMENT

Canoes are made from plastic, aluminum, wood, and other materials. Many canoes are made of fiberglass. This is a strong, lightweight material made by weaving threads of glass together. Some canoes are made from a combination of different materials. Vinyl, plastic, and foam combine to make a very flexible canoe. It springs back to shape if it crashes into a rock.

Canoes come in different styles. Those with flat bottoms are the most steady. They are suited for canoeists who prefer an easy paddle on calm water. Canoeists who want to go faster often use canoes with rounded bottoms. These are best for experienced canoeists because they are unsteady. Some canoes have V-shaped bottoms. These are the easiest to paddle in a straight line and are often used in canoe races.

One-Time Use

The first canoes were called dugouts. People hollowed out large tree trunks to make them. Dugouts were so heavy that paddlers often left them behind when they arrived at their destination.

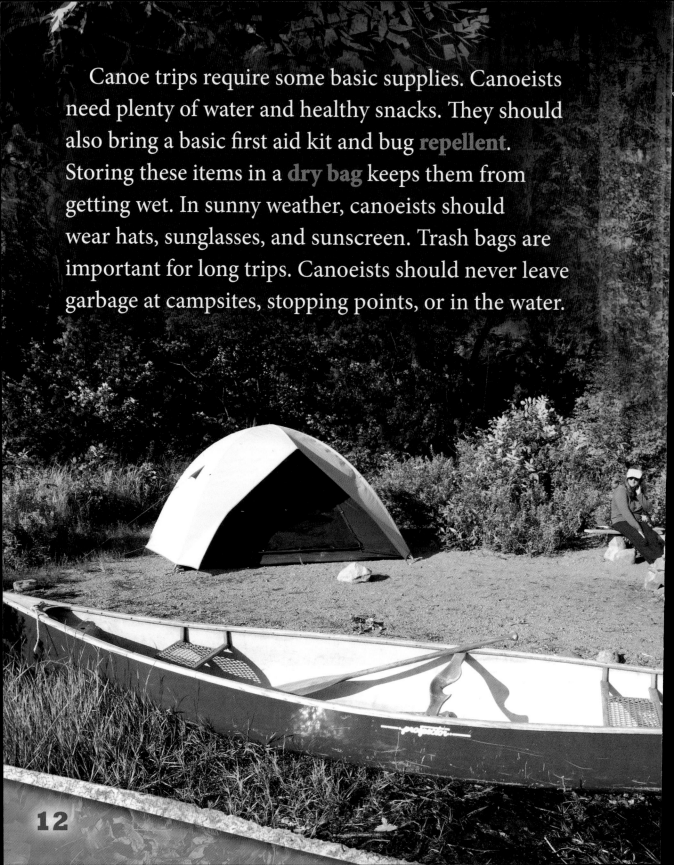

Canoe trips require some basic supplies. Canoeists need plenty of water and healthy snacks. They should also bring a basic first aid kit and bug repellent. Storing these items in a dry bag keeps them from getting wet. In sunny weather, canoeists should wear hats, sunglasses, and sunscreen. Trash bags are important for long trips. Canoeists should never leave garbage at campsites, stopping points, or in the water.

SKILLS AND SAFETY

Beginning canoeists should practice their skills on a quiet lake or slow-moving river. It is best if the water is protected from the wind and free of motorboats. It is safest to stay close to the shore.

Canoeing requires endurance, strength, and flexibility. Paddling is a repetitive motion that involves twisting the body. Many canoeists portage their heavy canoes across land. These people learn how to balance their canoes on their backs. They may portage their canoes and gear long distances over difficult terrain. This allows them to explore bodies of water that are not connected.

Basic Canoe Strokes

Forward Stroke
To move forward in a straight line

Put the blade in the water and move it from the front to the back of the canoe

Back Stroke
To stop or go in reverse

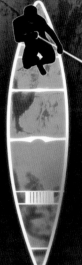

Put the blade in the water and move it from the back to the front of the canoe

Draw Stroke
To move sideways

Reach the blade out in the water and pull it back toward the canoe

Pry Stroke
To move sideways

Put the blade in the water under the canoe and push it away from the canoe

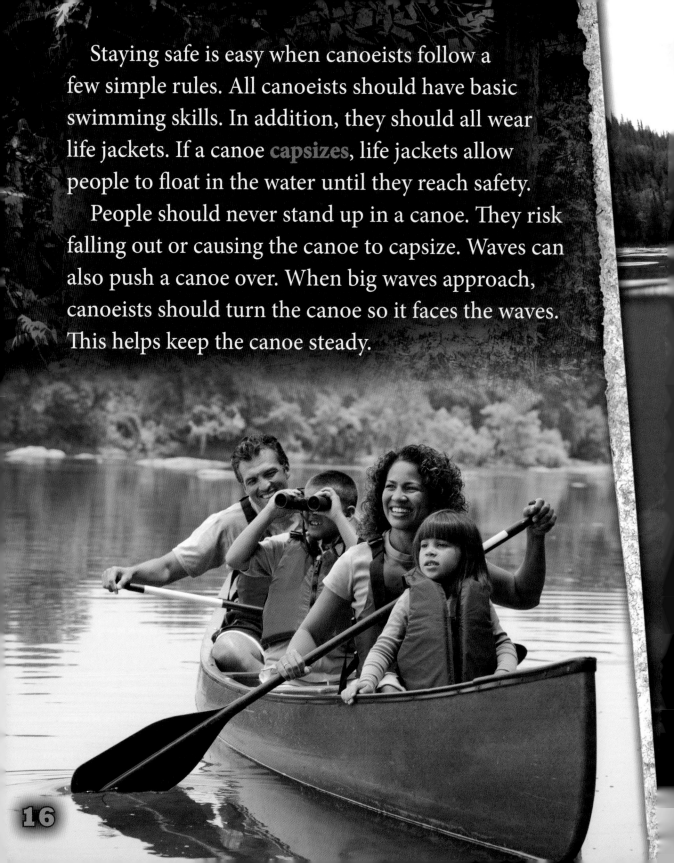

Staying safe is easy when canoeists follow a few simple rules. All canoeists should have basic swimming skills. In addition, they should all wear life jackets. If a canoe capsizes, life jackets allow people to float in the water until they reach safety.

People should never stand up in a canoe. They risk falling out or causing the canoe to capsize. Waves can also push a canoe over. When big waves approach, canoeists should turn the canoe so it faces the waves. This helps keep the canoe steady.

Canoeing Cleanup

Many people paddle canoes in river cleanup events. They scoop trash with nets as they move through the water.

Canoeists must know their physical limits. If they paddle too far one way, getting back can be difficult. It is also important to watch the weather. Heavy rain, lightning, and strong winds are dangerous to canoeists. Other threats are in the water. Fallen trees, rocks, and other obstacles can damage or trap a canoe.

Canoeing is a great way to experience the outdoors. People can glide across a lake or float down a river on a beautiful day. Canoeists with a spirit of adventure may choose to canoe through rapids or go on long-distance trips. Many people work with outfitters when they plan trips. Outfitters provide instruction, canoes, and equipment for people of all ages and skill levels.

Today, canoeing is one of the most popular water sports in the world. People canoe to relax, get exercise, and connect with nature. There is a lot to discover in a canoe!

MINNESOTA:
THE BOUNDARY WATERS
CANOE AREA

The Boundary Waters Canoe Area (BWCA) is a rugged wilderness area located on the border between Minnesota and Canada. It is often simply called the Boundary Waters. With over 1,000 lakes, the Boundary Waters is one of the best canoeing locations in the country. Canoeists can choose from more than 1,500 miles (2,414 kilometers) of canoe routes and 2,200 backcountry campsites. Most of these campsites can be reached only by water.

Visitors to the Boundary Waters must have permits. Canoeists can paddle on a single lake or canoe and portage across a chain of lakes. Wildlife is abundant in the Boundary Waters. Loons make their homes on many of the lakes. Canoeists might even spot moose, deer, beavers, and bears on the lakeshores. The Boundary Waters gives canoeists the chance to experience all that the Northwoods has to offer.

BWCA

GLOSSARY

aluminum—a lightweight silver metal

backcountry—wilderness; backcountry has little to no human development.

bow—the front part of a canoe

capsizes—tips over

dry bag—a waterproof bag; people put items they do not want to get wet in dry bags.

endurance—the ability to do something for a long time

outfitters—professionals who plan canoe trips and provide equipment and instruction for canoeists

permits—documents that give legal permission to do an activity

portage—to carry across land, often from one body of water to another

recreational—done for enjoyment

repellent—a substance used to keep something away

stern—the back part of a canoe

vinyl—a strong, flexible plastic often used as a covering

whitewater—rough, fast-moving water

TO LEARN MORE

At the Library

Salas, Laura Purdie. *Canoeing*. Mankato, Minn.: Capstone Press, 2008.

Westwood, Andrew. *Canoeing: The Essential Skills and Safety*. East Petersburg, Pa.: Heliconia Press, 2012.

Young, Jeff C. *Running the Rapids: White-Water Rafting, Canoeing, and Kayaking*. Edina, Minn.: ABDO Pub., 2011.

On the Web

Learning more about canoeing is as easy as 1, 2, 3.

1. Go to www.factsurfer.com.

2. Enter "canoeing" into the search box.

3. Click the "Surf" button and you will see a list of related Web sites.

With factsurfer.com, finding more information is just a click away.

INDEX

DATE DUE